Buy only what you need

The Disruptors'
Financial Plan
for
WEALTH

Ian Sender MBA
Warren Buffett as Your Investment Advisor

IAN Books

An IAN Books paperback

Published by
IAN Books
41 Watchung Plaza, B242
Montclair, NJ 07042

Copyright © 2018 IAN Books

All rights reserved. No part of this book or its Interactive Internet CD can be reproduced, transmitted in any form or by any means, electronic or mechanical, including photocopying, recording, or by any information storage and retrieval system, without the written permission of the publisher.

Cover photo: Isla en Guna Yala, Panamá by Ayaita

Special sales for educational use by nonprofits.
IANBooksEditor@yahoo.com

ISBN-13: 978-1720321538

ISBN-10: 1720321531

IAN Books at Amazon.com

Wealth Without Wall Street:
Buy Direct -- Avoid the Commissions, Fees, Loads

The Insiders' Guides to Buying Discount Financial Services:
Buy Direct and Save $3,000 Every Year

Drop Your Insurance:
Buy Only What You Need

Create Financial Freedom Using Your Wealth Reserve™:
Fix your financial life

The Simple Financial Life:
How to get what you want without going into debt and living paycheck to paycheck

Build Wealth Without Extra Money or Time:
You don't need to budget or get an extra job

Tax-FREE Retirement:
Use the tax code for lifetime income free of tax

The Working Millionaire:
$2,000,000 Tax-FREE Wealth Reserve ™ Self-insure Self-fund

Build Your Own $2,000,000 Tax-FREE Wealth Reserve™:
Self-insure Self-fund your lifestyle

Stop wasting $3,000 every year:
101
financial products ***NOT*** to buy and why

The DISRUPTORS' Plan

$1,100,000   5

1. Avoid income taxes.   9
2. Buffett's investment plan.   12
3. Compound stock earnings.   14
4. Buy buy buy investing.   17
5. Avoid high-fee managers.   19
6. Liar's Club: 'I can beat the market.'   20
7. Invest every month automatically.   23
8. Buy low-cost financial products.   25
9. Manage investments once a year.   27
10. Plan spending wisely.   28

    The DISRUPTORS help us build wealth   30

The Author   32

$1,100,000

This is the amount of money most of us say it takes to be "financially comfortable," according to a recent survey. However, only a few of us ever get there. Why?

    The main reason most of us are not 'comfortable' is that we don't *plan* to have a million dollars... ever. Most of us settle for a 'fantasy' $ million—playing the lottery every week. A $1 million is not hard to reach with a plan and TIME.

    Most of us do not have the essentials of a plan because we never learned about them. No one taught us. Our schools never taught us. Most of our parents couldn't teach us--they had no plan either. Even now pre-retirees lack vital knowledge.

    Now the DISRUPTORS of financial services have made it easier to gain the upper hand with an ***Essential Financial Plan***.

    Now we can create wealth for our family— $1,100,000 and more—by using new wealth-building tools from DISRUPTORS. We don't need expensive brokers, advisors or agents to buy the essentials of an efficient financial plan. We don't need a lot of money to start building wealth. All we need is TIME and a plan.

    First, we buy only what we need at discount prices. We don't pay high costs: fees, commissions, charges, expense ratios, bookkeeping, or add-ons. We keep more because we pay less. For instance, there are now many low-cost checking accounts, life insurance plans and wealth-building securities at cost.

    Second, over time, the stock market provides 10-12% returns a year. Now we don't have to pay 1-3% a year in order to grow our money. In the past we gave up over 50% of our nest egg:

        $3,000 per year @11%   for 33 years = $1,018,177
        $3,000 per year @11-1% for 33 years = $778,768
        $3,000 per year @11-2% for 33 years = $613,805
        $3,000 per year @11-3% for 33 years = $486,634

Third, you can earn 11% on your long-term money and end up with a million dollars or more with one phone call. You do not need an advisor or learn how to pick stocks. That is the fastest way to *lose* money. The average advisor-assisted investor earned just 3.79% instead of the market rate of 11%. Dalbar's QAIB.

Instead of paying commissions and high fees, we use the strategy proven by **Warren Buffett**, the greatest investor of our time. Playing the market by trading stocks and timing the market gyrations is the Loser's Game according to research.

We beat Wall Street at their own game by using Warren Buffett's strategy: buy and keep buying the largest mutual funds run at cost and owned by us, the investors. We can't afford hedge funds, offshore tax shelters, and expensive Wall Street money managers taking 1-3% a year. We are not as smart as Mr Buffett.

A plain market index fund beat 92-95% of the returns of "professional" managers, including hedge funds. Stock picking by geniuses only works for a short time. Insiders may have an edge but it is illegal and you could get caught like Martha Stewart did.

To earn more, we pay as little as we can. We own stocks of companies with certain characteristics. We Pay Less; Get More. We use a special investment account to eliminate all future income and capital gains taxes. It is IRS-approved for workers.

This is the strategy our 'advisor' Warren Buffett recommends. We beat the 'professionals' at their own game. Instead of trading stocks, we buy more of them when the price is low and fewer when it is high. No one can time the market well.

We don't pay Wall Street owners the $1.3 Trillion per year revenues they take from clients now. If you think you need financial help, pay for a one-time session, not quarterly fees taking 2% of your account every year.

Your current advisor is costing you real money. The average return for managed accounts is 3.79%. A low-cost index fund provides 11%. You are giving up 63% of your total potential earnings. You can do better on your own with the DISRUPTORS. 'Advisors' weave fantasy stories about investing to trick you into giving them your money. Do you really think an expert at selling knows anything about what will happen to a security or the market in the next hour, week or year? Sales people only sell.

> "My wealth has come from a combination of living in America, some lucky genes, and **compound interest**."

Buffett says, The real secret to investing is **compounding**. You can earn $1,000,000 with $250 a month over time in the market or just $208,000 with advisor average of 3.79%. Your choice.

Low-cost stock mutual funds are our only viable long-term asset over time. Other assets have lower or more volatile returns. If you have 10 years until you need money, stocks give "purchasing power" to beat inflation especially for investors under age 65.

Selling and buying in our account kills Buffett's strategy for wealth—*compounding*: Vanguard's 500 index return: 10.97% since 1976. All we have to do is buy and hold low-cost funds.

Forget 'safe' or 'sound' investment advice. Ignore products pitched to 'sophisticated' investors like 'private placement' and special backtested formulas. Ignore friends/family advice: Madoff's fake returns drew thousands by word of mouth.

Until recently, if you wanted to participate in the market—earn more than bank rates—you had no choice but to pay dearly. Most small savers could not afford to buy securities. More importantly, our schools did not teach us how and where to invest. They did not show us that wealth comes from the *power of compounding* over time.

I will show how your family can grow your savings to a $ million or more. An hour online or by phone is all you need to set up a TAX-FREE account with no brokerage fees or commissions. The less you pay the more you keep. And no taxes!

The wealthy have figured out how to avoid taxes. For instance, Warren Buffett, with $90 billions, pays only 17% **total** tax: http://www.youtube.com/watch?v=Cu5B-2LoC4s; Mitt Romney only **14%**; John Kerry only **13%** and Apple just **9.8%**. Buffett found that his staff pays **32.9%**—DOUBLE his rate!

You set up a tax-FREE account with the largest mutual fund company. You will have that company's trustee invest your automatic bank debit once a month. You do nothing else—No trading; No market timing; No speculation; *TIME, not timing*.

When I got my securities licenses, I investigated the various strategies made famous by Lynch, O'Shaughnessy, O'Neil, Dreman, Neff, Zweig, Fisher, Graham, Buffett, and 'Dogs of Dow.' I tried some of these stock screens to find winning equities. I tried trading to time the market's ups and downs. I used 3 online discount brokerages over time so I did not have to pay for commissions at my own firm.

After all this work and expense, it was hard to know if I made more than the market returns. Like most investors, I held one stock too long expecting it to rebound. I lost.

It is a tragedy that this industry does not allow our high schools to teach investing for the long-term. At the same time, it was not until recently that it became easy for working people to invest the right way. I learned to invest with the DISRUPTORS not with the 'professionals' of my firm.

John Bogle created Vanguard mutual funds. When I worked on Wall Street, I never heard about Vanguard's unique investing solution. He began in 1976.

Bogle realized that costs determine success in investing. Vanguard provides us with the opportunity to buy mutual funds DIRECTLY from the manufacturer. Vanguard is owned by us, its investors. We get our securities *at cost*. Profits are returned as annual fee reductions: Lower than the for-profit industry.

Bogle created the first consumer index fund. You do not need to try to pick the "needle" in the haystack, he says. The chance of your advisor identifying the next Apple or Google is 1 in 19,000. Because there are so many variables that we can't determine as a company grows, it is almost impossible to pick, in advance, the one that beats the market *over time*. We can pick the TIME we spend in the market not the one blockbuster stock.

Warren Buffett shared his strategy of building assets. He buys, on sale, stocks of companies we all use and holds them "forever." We acknowledge that no one can pick the next Apple or Google so we buy and hold funds with the stocks of companies that have the 'longevity gene.'

Use the The DISRUPTORS to help you provide wealth for your family.

Avoid income taxes

Bogle, Buffett and William Roth are DISRUPTORS. Part of the Wall Street herd bias is trading which produces taxes for you, not for your advisor. One of the strategies of the wealthy is to avoid taxes on their accumulations. Consider the examples I provided above: Buffett pays just **17%**, Romney **14%**, Kerry **13%** and Apple **9.8%**. Most of the top 1% pay far less than the average citizen of this country in terms of disposable income.

If the average family earns $85,000, they pay about 14% federal, 13% SS/Med/UC/Health, 10% state/local, 4% sales/excise, or over 30% total taxes. As Buffett said, "I pay 17.7% total tax. My office staff pays 32.9%." Of course this does not include pension and other insurance deductions most Americans also pay.

This is why the wealthy avoid taxes with their own businesses and various tax-advantaged vehicles. In order to become and stay wealthy, people need to have money to invest. The average family has little extra money to build wealth let alone have enough for retirement. They need tax-FREE compounding.

The following graph makes clear that in order to accumulate $1,000,000 from monthly contributions, we must buy and hold the securities of growing companies worldwide AND pay **zero** tax on the growth to *maximize compounding*. We can see clearly that investing in growing company stocks is more likely to get us to our goal in our lifetime than investing in government bonds or a bank savings account.

As your investments grow—especially mutual funds that pay dividends and gains each year—you will not have to pay tax on them because of your special IRS-approved account. Most regular IRAs and pension accounts are tax-DEFERRED *not* tax-FREE. Taxes have to be paid sometime.

Disruptor: William Roth. Your Roth IRA allows you to leverage tax-FREE accumulations over time against an immediate tax deduction as with a regular IRA or 401k pension. The benefits can be enormous. For instance, if you make contributions of $250 a month, $3,000 a year to your low-cost stock mutual funds, you could spend $30,000 tax-FREE for every $3,000 you deposited!

Invest $250 a month, $3000 a year, never pay tax

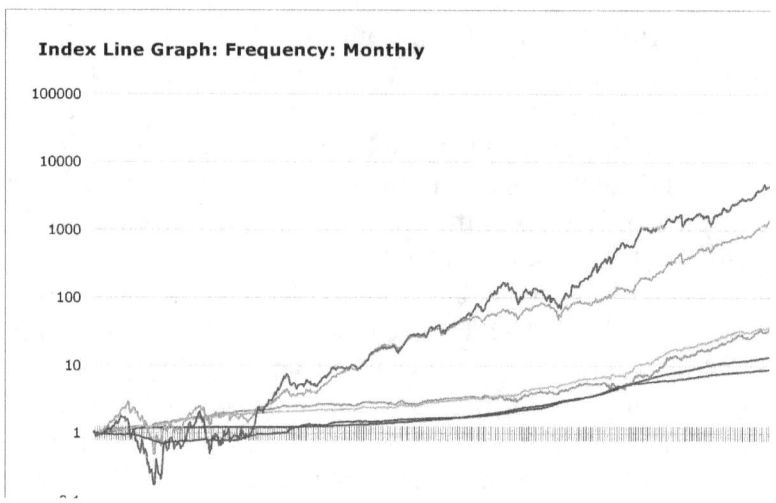

Top line—Small Cap Stocks
2nd line—Large Cap Stocks (S&P 500)
3rd line—US Long-term Corporate Bonds
4th line—Intermediate-term Government Bonds
5th line—US 30 day Government T-bills
6th line—US inflation
Courtesy: Dr. Campbell R. Harvey http://www.duke.edu/~charvey/

The Roth IRA Rules

Contributions:

$5,500 ($6,500 over age 50) each year
Income under $135,000 (2018) single
married $199,000 (2018)

Distributions:

Tax-FREE for contributions.
And Tax-FREE for earnings if
Over age 59 1/2,
Account open 5 years,
Taxable earnings unless
Disabled,
First home ($10,000),
Death

Bonus:

Account can grow tax-FREE for life
Minimum distribution rules don't apply
Heirs don't pay income tax
Account has no maximum

Check with your tax preparer
https://www.irs.gov/pub/irs-pdf/p590a.pdf

Buffett's investment plan

The rules for the use of your Roth IRA account are manageable by you. You don't need an advisor. The rules are found at https://www.irs.gov/retirement-plans/roth-iras. Your account trustee can answer most questions. You don't need to pay an attorney. All of the large low-cost mutual funds firms are trustees. I will discuss the best firms available below.

You can start this account with any of the firms with no upfront charges. Most charge an annual fee for the bookkeeping. We will consider the specific investment options later. We will use low-cost firms because you will keep more of your own money. You don't need to pay Wall Street to maintain this account.

It is important to pick a trustee with the least costs since over time the annual costs can really destroy your accumulations. For instance, if you use a brokerage firm, you might pay 2-3% of your balance annually. You could give up 63% of your earnings. If both spouses have a low-cost account with contributions of $250 a month for 27 years, they could accumulate $1,000,000. If they use a high-cost broker/advisor, both accounts may hit only $282,000. Depending on earnings of 8-10% and total costs of 2% per year, you could really hurt yourself. You need to watch the costs. Advisors do NOT beat the markets over the long term. Just stick with your Buffett investment plan.

You can open your account at any age as long as you have *earned* income—paper route too. Stock dividends or interest do not count. Any job will do. You don't even need a job requiring a W-2 to prove it. A part-time, weekend or night job will do. Any cash-only work will qualify—even for a child. Accountants recommend that receipts and records be maintained. You could even work for yourself in a home-office business like I do.

Nontaxable distributions from a Roth IRA won't affect your eligibility for student aid either. Later, in retirement, this money won't affect your social security benefits as of the rules today.

The *Miracle of Compounding* works.

Actual client Tom's account, investing $250 a month, 1962-2003

Return	Balance
24%	3,720
16%	7,795
12%	12,091
-10%	13,582
24%	20,561
11%	26,153
-8%	26,821
4%	31,013
14%	38,775
19%	49,713
-14%	45,333
-26%	35,766
37%	53,110
24%	69,576
-8%	66,770
6%	73,956
18%	90,809
32%	123,827
-5%	120,486
22%	150,653
21%	185,920
6%	200,255
32%	268,297
19%	322,843
5%	342,135
17%	403,808
32%	536,987
-3%	523,787
31%	690,091
8%	748,538
10%	826,692
2%	846,286
38%	1,172,015
23%	1,445,268
33%	1,926,197
28%	2,469,372
21%	2,991,570
-9%	2,725,059
-12%	2,403,420
-22%	1,874,601
29%	2,412,905

Compound stock earnings

Compounding high earnings is your *best* strategy. The wealthy get richer just by leaving their money invested. They don't work more hours or take more risks. The famous 1% at the top of society take down 23.5% of all income (up from 8.9% 30 years ago). They don't work any harder than you do—*their money does*.

    Because of compounding, many millionaires have said, "the first million was the hardest." It takes a working business person about 34 years to grow $250 a month to $1,000,000 using tax-advantaged investments. However, it only takes 7-9 years to double their money to $2 million. Investors in stock funds, earning 10-12% on average, can double it again to $4 million in less than 10 years without adding new money. Their tax-advantaged accounts make it easier to reach their goal. It is compounding that makes it happen—not Wall Street brokerage fees.

    Compounding of high earnings means that we make money on our last period's accumulations. The progression looks like the client's account values on the previous page. Notice that our balance can double in a couple of good years. This happens because we are not just adding $3,000 per year, but adding up to 38% of the previous year's accumulation to our balance. We are making money on top of our money with no extra effort on our part. During this 40 year period, this client lost money some years. In fact, they lost 14% and then 26% back to back, but then made 37% and 24%.

    Wealthy people don't panic. They have learned that compounding over the long-term is the only way they can build wealth. There are no successful get-rich-quick schemes. To reach their goal, they know there will be setbacks. No business grows steadily upward all the time. They have seen the losses before and they don't sell their assets in a panic.

    We will buy <u>assets that "grow by themselves</u>." We will have security because our ***purchasing power*** will grow over time. We begin with a fund with 500 large company stocks. We earn 10-12% and then buy all ten Vanguard funds over time reducing our risk of owning just one fund. When one fund is down, others are up.

The Vanguard Top Ten

2017 Total Return	Fund	Long-term Return	Longevity
21.7%	500 Index	11.1%*	since 1976
3.2%	Energy	10.7%	since 1984
17.9%	Extended Market	10.9%	since 1987
19.6%	Health	16.5%	since 1984
42.9%	International Growth	10.8%	since 1981
29.5%	PRIMECAP	13.9%	since 1984
16.1%	Small Cap Index	10.7%	since 1960
10.2%	Wellesley Income	9.9%	since 1970
19.1%	Windsor	11.5%	since 1958
16.8%	Windsor II	10.8%	since 1985
19.7%	Average	11.7%	

*Average Annual Returns as of 12/31/17.

This kind of security comes from our regular contributions ... and patience. The miracle of compounding works its magic on our Roth IRA account when we give it TIME. The wealthy give their money time to compound. They don't take it out and they try not to pay tax every year on the gains. They maintain their contribution schedule because each $100 added is worth $10,000 to them later. They use the compound interest calculator so they know the future value: moneychimp.com/calculator/compound_interest_calculator.htm.

Most people who become wealthy have to wait for years of slow growth in their account. It took client Tom 21 years to get to $150,000. Then it only took 14 years to get to a $1,172,015. After only 4 years, it became $3,000,000. Shortly thereafter he "lost" over a million dollars!

This client stuck with it and was successful in reaching the goal but there are many who do not. Most people who are not wealthy already, have a hard time believing it can happen with only their *patience*. They just don't have the experience of how compounding works to keep faith in its outcome eventually.

Once an account becomes sizable, we don't need to add contributions to it. Usually, by the time we stop regular employment, we aren't making contributions. Some wealthy people continue to work after age 65 because they love what they do and want to continue. Obviously, they don't need to work. The **miracle of compounding** continues to work.

The annual returns of growing companies

2016 Total Return	Fund	Long-term Return	Longevity
11.9%	500 Index	10.9%*	since 1976
33.1%	Energy	10.9%	since 1984
16.1%	Extended Market	10.7%	since 1987
-9.0%	Health	16.4%	since 1984
1.7%	International Growth	10.0%	since 1981
10.7%	PRIMECAP	13.4%	since 1984
18.3%	Small Cap Index	10.7%	since 1960
8.1%	Wellesley Income	9.9%	since 1970
12.5%	Windsor	11.3%	since 1958
13.4%	Windsor II	10.7%	since 1985
11.7%	Average	11.5%	

*Average Annual Returns as of 12/31/16.

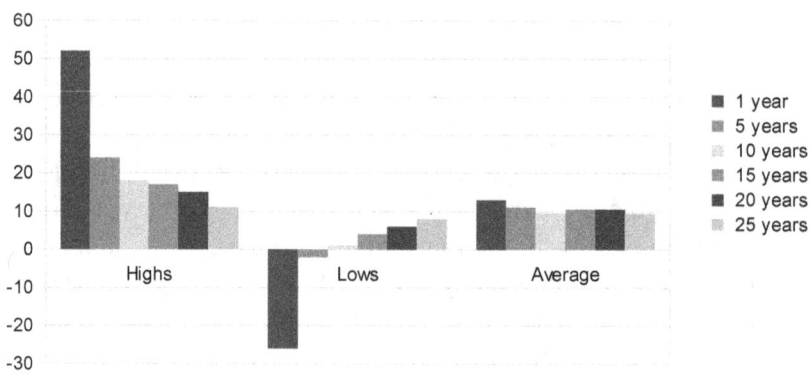

Range of annual returns of stocks, 1950 – 2000

Buy buy buy investing

When we develop the ***habit*** of investing, we take our emotions out of the process. We, as a silent partner, must learn to live with the market downs. We need to think of this account as our stake in growing businesses as they go up and down. See page 13.

It is easier to be patient if we make contributions automatic. Like the Social Security contributions we make every payday, the contributions come out of our bank automatically. We can have the Roth IRA trustee debit our checking account automatically every month. Businesses grow in spurts. We must hold on.

As one client told us, "I never see the deduction, so I never miss it." Of course this client has already identified the $250 he has committed to his $1,000,000 future. He took our advice and went through his spending on financial services. He used our Guides to find the $250 a month he was wasting on products and services he would never use or need. In our amazon.com/Insiders-Guides-Discount-Financial-Services/ you will find "**tricks of the trade**" that we insiders use to buy directly from quality manufacturers for less.

It's easy to say **I will start later.** Starting 5 years later means ending up with HALF the amount we were shooting for. It is hard to believe that missing that $250 a month for 5 years or $15,000 can reduce our total from $600,000 to $300,000.

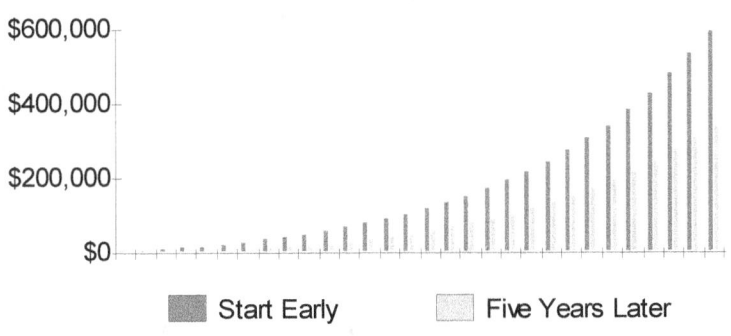

Your investment plan over time

$2,000 Annual Stock Market Investment 1950- '70- '80- '90- 2013

Year	Returns	Balance	Balance	Balance	Balance
		$2,000			
1950	31%	$2,620			
1951	24%	$5,729			
1952	18%	$9,120			
1953	-1%	$11,009			
1954	52%	$19,773			
1955	31%	$28,523			
1956	5%	$32,049			
1957	-11%	$30,304			
1958	43%	$46,194			
1959	12%	$53,978			
1960	1%	$56,538			
1961	26%	$73,757			
1962	-8%	$69,697			
1963	24%	$88,904			
1964	16%	$105,449			
1965	12%	$120,342			
1966	-10%	$110,108			
1967	24%	$139,014			
1968	11%	$156,526			
1969	-8%	$145,844	2,000		
1970	4%	$153,757	2,080		
1971	14%	$177,563	4,651		
1972	19%	$213,681	7,915		
1973	-14%	$185,485	8,527		
1974	-26%	$138,739	7,790		
1975	37%	$192,813	13,412		
1976	24%	$241,568	19,111		
1977	-8%	$224,082	19,422		
1978	6%	$239,647	22,707		
1979	18%	$285,144	29,155	2,000	
1980	32%	$379,030	41,124	2,640	
1981	-5%	$361,978	40,968	4,408	
1982	22%	$444,053	52,421	7,818	
1983	21%	$539,724	65,850	11,879	
1984	6%	$574,228	71,921	14,712	
1985	32%	$760,621	97,575	22,060	
1986	19%	$907,519	118,494	28,632	
1987	5%	$954,995	126,519	32,163	
1988	17%	$1,119,684	150,367	39,971	
1989	32%	$1,480,623	201,125	55,402	2,000
1990	-3%	$1,438,144	197,031	55,680	1,940
1991	31%	$1,886,589	260,731	75,560	5,161
1992	8%	$2,039,676	283,749	83,765	7,734
1993	10%	$2,245,843	314,324	94,342	10,708
1994	2%	$2,292,800	322,651	98,268	12,962
1995	38%	$3,166,824	448,018	138,370	20,647
1996	23%	$3,897,654	553,522	172,656	27,856
1997	33%	$5,186,540	738,844	232,292	39,709
1998	28%	$6,641,331	948,281	299,894	53,387
1999	21%	$8,038,430	1,149,839	365,291	67,019
2000	-9%	$7,316,791	1,048,174	334,235	62,807
2001	-12%	$6,447,855	925,203	296,223	57,095
2002	-22%	$5,024,437	722,291	232,316	46,035
2003	29%	$6,459,474	930,787	301,119	61,730
2004	11%	$7,164,483	1,034,274	336,099	70,664
2005	5%	$7,512,677	1,084,540	352,433	74,098
2006	15%	$8,694,884	1,259,259	412,409	90,450
2007	5%	$9,163,538	1,327,133	434,638	95,325
2008	-39%	$5,601,431	813,388	268,074	60,754
2009	27%	$7,116,358	952,155	342,993	79,699
2010	15%	$8,186,112	1,097,278	396,742	93,954
2011	2%	$8,347,378	1,118,894	404,558	95,805
2012	16%	$9,666,264	1,295,679	468,478	110,942
2013	32%	$12,759,468	1,710,296	618,390	146,443
Avg.	12%	12%	11%	13%	11%

I.A.N. LLC © 2014   1/2/14   TheInsidersGuides.com

Ibbotson Associates **Stocks average 11.4% per year, bonds 5%, CDs 3%.** Stocks have gone up as much as 54% and as low as –43% in 1 year, up to 28% or down to –12% in 5 years, up 20% or down 0% in 10 years, up 18% or up 3% in 20 years. Short term bonds have gone up 14% or up 0% in 1 year, up 11% or up 0% in 5 years, up 9% or up 0% in 10 years, up 10% or up 1% in 20 years.

Avoid "high-fee managers"

**"In every single time period and data point tested,
low-cost funds beat high-cost funds."**

According to an unbiased Morningstar study, low-cost funds beat high-cost funds PERIOD. However, the myth of Wall Street is that you must pay more for good performance. Warren Buffett's mentor, Benjamin Graham, advised: "buy financial products like we buy "groceries, ... not perfume."

The best predictor of your investing and wealth building success is **low cost**. When we subtract the costs of buying and maintaining investments, we give up a lot of the gains. A stock fund that reflects the overall market is called an index fund. This kind of fund costs only 0.04% ($4 per $10,000). Our account will compound at or near the 10-12% trend over time.

The chart below makes it clear. Over time, the advisor costs we pay each year will cut our total accumulation by up to 63%. Instead of compounding at 10-12% annually on average, some people give up 1.5-3% of the earnings on their money to the middle person. They end up with less.

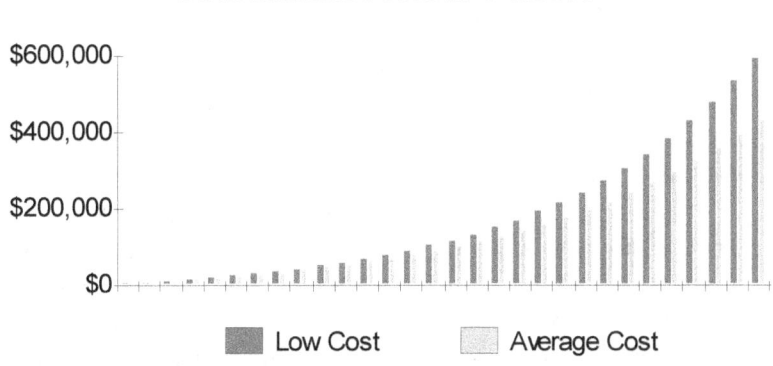

Low-cost index funds beat 95% of funds with a stock-picking manager. Wall Street takes $ 1.3 Trillion of our money in fees.

Liar's Club: 'I can beat the market'

__Liar's Poker__ is a game author Michael Lewis says traders play when they get bored. It involves bluffing. But when your advisor or money manager does it to you, it's fraud. When retail customers don't know how and where to invest properly, sales people make up stories. They don't lie exactly; they mislead. Sales people only survive if they <u>separate you from your money</u> or your potential earnings. Fact: You need a plan that takes only one hour to follow.

    Picking ***individual*** stocks as a strategy is not likely to work for us. Professional managers and day traders have had limited success <u>over time</u>. Our strategy is to build wealth as a silent partner in growing global companies. Since it is unlikely that we (or anyone else) will be able to pick the next Google or Apple, we invest in a large group of firms. We do not need to fear picking the wrong one or picking one at the wrong time. As the founder of the largest mutual fund firm, John Bogle, says: "Don't look for the needle. Buy the haystack." This is a proven successful strategy.

    A mutual fund manager advertises that their fund has "beaten" the market and so we pay 1.5-3% of our assets every year. Over time we find that while the stock market index rose **11.06%**, we earned only **3.79%** annually. In this way, costs can take 63% of our returns over time. Each time they sell and buy, we give up some of our compound earnings.

    When young investors begin investing, they cannot buy all 10 Vanguard funds listed above at once with $250 per month. Vanguard has minimums on all funds so they can keep their expenses low for everyone.

    There are two ways to start our Roth IRA account. The easiest way is to save $250 a month in our savings account until we have the $1,000 minimum for Vanguard's entry fund: STAR #56. We can open the Roth IRA by phone or <u>online</u>: <u>STAR</u> minimum is $1,000. Most Vanguard funds need $3,000 to start. We can keep contributing to the STAR fund until we have $3,000 for the 500 Index and then $3,000 for the Extended Market funds and eventually all 10 funds. Vanguard is at 800.551.8631.

    The second way to begin is to open a Roth IRA at TIAA, the world's largest pension company, primarily for educational and research institutions. Low expenses and low initial contributions make TIAA an organization we can stay with. TIAA 800.842.2888.

At TIAA we can make application and begin immediately with an automatic monthly contribution of $100 or more from our bank account. We can follow how the assets grow by themselves. TIAA has two funds that provide us with the diversity of companies worldwide: TIAA Equity Index and TIAA International Equity.

Request a prospectus (owner's manual) for each fund you will be using at Vanguard or TIAA. Both mutual fund firms have experienced salaried representatives that provide accurate information about accounts and funds. Both offer low-cost index funds that hold a broad representation of the market returns of 10-12%. This is a building block to accumulating wealth.

Both firms are focused on you, not on profits.

Our strategy is to buy mutual funds with stocks of growing companies worldwide. No Wall Street guru can predict the future winners. Most can't do better than 50%—a flip of the coin. Your investments provide long-term growth of 10-12% annually on average with the benefit of avoiding single company or industry failures. It provides exposure to new growth potential around the world with less risk than holding one company, one sector, or one country. Some years our account is up 33% and some years down 22%. However, we double our money every 7-9 years *over time.*

How does your investment grow? Time is the key. Take as example your payday contributions to Social Security. A couple pays in 6.2% of salary. It is matched by the employer. Baby Boomers who made average salaries all their lives are now taking benefits of about $1,500 each--$36,000 a year. Because benefits are pegged to inflation, they may receive $1,260,000 during the rest of their lives. And SS contributions are NOT invested in the stock market index.

Our investments earn 10-12% a year while contributions are NOT even invested in the stock market index.

It is the amount we KEEP that matters!

Monthly	Accumulation at 12% per year									
	5	10	15	20	25	30	35	40	45	50
$100	$8,167	$23,004	$49,958	$98,925	$187,884	$349,496	$643,095	$1,176,477	$2,145,469	$3,905,834
$200	$16,334	$46,008	$99,916	$197,850	$375,768	$698,992	$1,286,190	$2,352,954	$4,290,938	$7,811,668
$300	$24,501	$69,012	$149,874	$296,775	$563,652	$1,048,488	$1,929,285	$3,529,431	$6,436,408	$11,717,502
$500	$40,835	$115,020	$249,790	$494,625	$939,420	$1,747,480	$3,215,475	$5,882,385	$10,727,346	$19,529,169

. . .

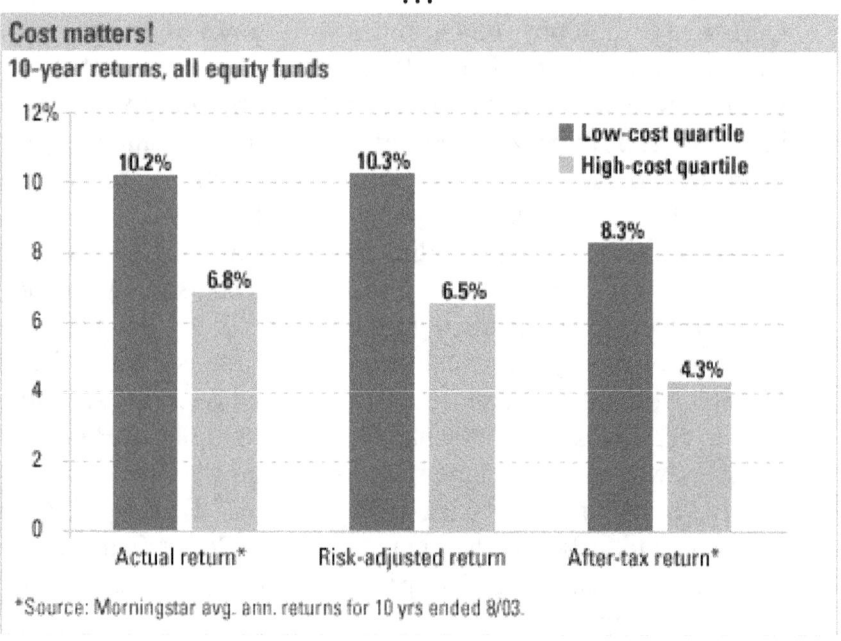

*Source: Morningstar avg. ann. returns for 10 yrs ended 8/03.

Invest every month automatically

We need to find at least $250 per month to invest in order to build our account. We can build wealth by following the strategy outlined in the previous chapters, but we need to have at least 10% of income available to invest. In my experience, it doesn't matter how much people earn, most say they don't have the money to invest for their future. "Today is hard enough," they complain.

Yes, that may well be, but if we don't find the $250, for example, we won't have a very happy tomorrow. We have to go back to our goal. We want to build wealth: accumulating $1,000,000 over time. Based on the way wealth compounds, we need to invest at least $250 a month, every month. We need to be consistent for the **miracle of compounding** to work.

A Spending Plan is a way to set priorities for our regular spending. We can accumulate $1 million to accomplish all that we want to do in life by using just 10 percent of our income to buy assets that "grow by themselves." We don't run the firms we own.

Using a Spending Plan is **like brushing your teeth**—it's a habit that isn't that difficult to learn—then it is automatic. Our Spending Plan must include what we need to function now and in the future. Like building a business, it takes planning and following the steps we talked about so far.

Some investors include the $250 in their automatic bill payment or have the trustee debit their account automatically. Others set up family goals and decide to put a certain amount in a separate account for each goal. In this way, they keep the wealth building process in the forefront of their monthly bill payments.

Whatever way works for you. The important thing is to change the status of wealth building from a vague future desire to a monthly habit. "Set it and forget it" is the theme of investing.

Most people find that the easiest way is to set up an automatic debit of their checking account by the trustee at the time of the application for the Roth IRA. If we are using a Roth 401k or an employer account, we set up the retirement account with automatic contributions. We are less likely to quit if a trustee debits monthly.

Some people are successful by making a written plan. They

have some idea of how much they will need at some time in the future. The account is set up as a Roth IRA so the **contributions** are not taxed when used before age 59.5. After that age, there are no taxes at all—EVER.

Another benefit of using a Spending Plan is that we become focused on how we spend our money. We are more inclined to buy only what we need. For financial services, we 'insiders' compiled the ***The Insiders Guides*** for each area—insurance, securities, etc. They provide an easy way to save $3,000 or more on financial products we already use. This is where we buy discount products.

We can't build wealth by spending more than we earn. Building wealth takes patience and commitment to contributing to our investment business every month. Some people don't try to be disciplined investors. They let the trustee debit the $250 or 10% every month so they can't fail to become a millionaire.

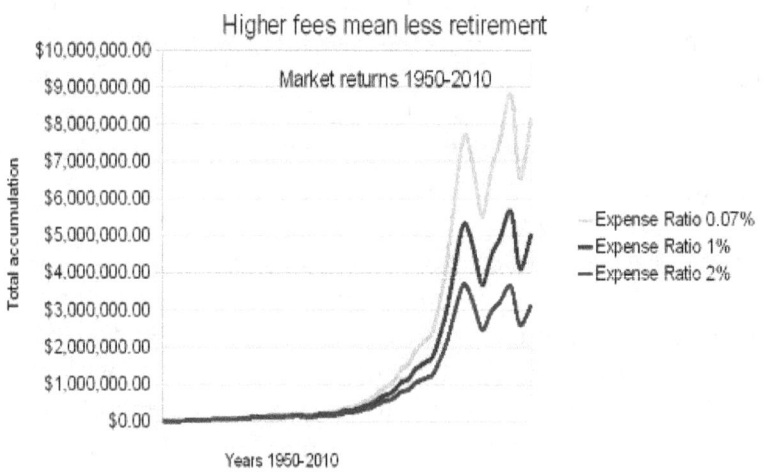

Are you paying too much?

Buy low-cost financial products

Disruptor: John Bogle invented the low-cost mutual fund cooperative structure that allows us to accumulate stock earnings at cost—No middle person or profit firm to take a large chunk of our earnings. It is not picking stocks but *time* that builds wealth.

It is easy to build wealth if we already have a pile of money. But how do we capture that first $500,000, that $250,000, or even that first $50,000? It comes from buying assets that 'grow by themselves.' It takes time for the companies we own through your fund to produce earnings. As Buffett just proved, the easiest way to make sure we reach our goal of a million dollars is to buy low-cost index fund shares *automatically NOT THROUGH A BROKER.*

But where do we get the $250 a month? The best way is to "REDIRECT" the **cash we already spend** on things we really don't need or can buy for less. This is how millionaires stay millionaires. They don't over pay!

Most working people waste $3,000 or more each year on financial services. We must shop for financials like we shop for groceries: buy the house brand and use discounts. For instance, the difference between paying full price for a new car and a 3-year-old model can be 40% or more.

There are DISRUPTORS selling every financial need for less:

Auto insurance: save $400 or more EVERY year by changing/dropping some benefits we don't need.

Home insurance: save $200 or more EVERY year by changing one limit.

Life insurance: save $1,000 or more EVERY year by using direct to consumer term insurer.

Mutual funds: save $2-3,000 EVERY year by using low-cost providers.

Bank: save $120 EVERY year by using a low-cost provider of the benefits we usually use. Credit Union.

Mortgage: save $2,000 on closings and lower interest rates.

Investments: earn 15-30% guaranteed just by paying off credit cards.

Growth mutual funds: save up to 50% over time.

Tax refund: Averages $3,022 and usually spent.

Using our ***The Insiders' Guides to Buying Discount Financial Services: Buy Direct and Save $3,000 Every Year,*** we can uses the DISRUPTORS to redirect $250 a month without having to give up anything. We don't need to tighten our belt or make a budget. We can give up things we would not benefit from anyway.

Best example: MetLife charged $983 for a $300,000 30-year **term policy**. This same $300,000 benefit was sold by Savings Bank Life Insurance for $384 a year. Their financial strength ratings are A+ and their underwriting requirements are the same. The difference, $599, over 30 years is $17,970. If invested, this difference can add $175,000 to OUR **account**.

This strategy—to cut out the middle people who are taking your money with little benefit to you—makes sense and works! But the most important part of our strategy is keep investing: ***buying more shares of mutual funds when they are 'on sale.'***

2011 Total Return	Fund	Long-term Return*	Longevity
1.97%	500 Index	10.36%	since 1976
-1.74%	Energy	12.71%	since 1984
-3.73%	Extended Market	9.96%	since 1987
11.45%	Health	16.30%	since 1984
-13.68%	International Growth	10.50%	since 1981
-1.84%	PRIMECAP	12.79%	since 1984
-2.80%	Small Cap Index	10.26%	since 1960
9.63%	Wellesley Income	10.16%	since 1970
-4.00%	Windsor	11.00%	since 1958
2.70%	Windsor II	10.18%	since 1985
0.00%	Average	11.42%	

*Average Annual Returns as of 12/31/11.

We must ignore what others are doing when some markets fall because we are gaining more shares NOT cashing in at panic prices. Just remember George Bailey's during the 1929 panic:

Potter isn't selling. Potter's buying! And why? Because we're panicky and he's not. That's why. He's pickin' up some bargain. Now, we can get through this thing all right. We've, we've got to stick together, though. We've got to have faith in each other. ***It's a Wonderful Life***

Manage investments once a year

"We continue to make more money when *snoring* than when active."

Disruptor: Warren Buffett gave us this advice. As the most successful investor of our day we should listen. He is making it clear that we should NOT touch our investments very often. We buy shares of the top companies and hold them all our lives—selling them only for our retirement income.

Wall Street makes money on transactions. So don't trade. We ignore the market and keep buying so we end up with $1 million. When the market is down we keep our mind on the graph on p. 17. We have to remember Warren Buffett's advice and hold on to stocks/stock funds. In fact, Mr Buffett says "**our favorite holding period is forever.**" http://www.berkshirehathaway.com/letters/1988.html

Even if the market drops; it will rise. It fell 22% in 2002 and rose 29% in 2003. We only have to look at our tax-FREE account once a year. We make sure we are making contributions to the specific mutual fund that is down for the year. We don't 'rebalance.'

When we first started investing, we use the STAR Index. After we had accumulated enough to buy the 500 Index ($3,000), we trade shares of the STAR Index and buy it. We keep investing into the 500 Index until we have the minimum for the next one. We repeat this pattern until we have the minimum in each. Then we add to the one that is down for the year. Repeat each year.

As we accumulate the minimum for each fund, then transfer into the next one, we do not need to pay tax on the sale because we are using a tax-FREE Roth IRA. This is part of the **miracle of compounding**. After accumulating a large proportion of our goal, adding the $250 per month does not matter to the outcome. We can borrow to pay for cars, vacation, other goals. For instance, our client whose account is shown on page 13 took $25,000 for a used luxury car in the year the account hit over half a million. His account total did not suffer long term.

Managing investments once a year is wise advice. Our tax-FREE account does not require us to hire an advisor to manage it.

We have the *power of compounding* so we don't need advisors.

Plan spending wisely

We own the 10 funds to build wealth. We have learned to be patient and accumulate $1,000,000 or more. We have paid back any amounts that we borrowed to pay cash for large purchases. We have been fortunate that the historical averages of market returns have produced the accumulations we set as our goals.

NOW WHAT?

Now we can take 6-8% out of the account each year and pay no income taxes. As of 2017, most states follow the IRS code on our **account**, a Roth IRA. https://www.irs.gov/retirement-plans/roth-iras

Many people move 60% of their money into a balanced fund like the Wellesley Income fund. It has produced over 9% per year on average since 1970. They created a retirement spending plan that assured them of that monthly income of a fixed dollar amount with this Guide. amazon.com/Your-Retirement-Spending-Plan-enough.

We have created our $1,000,000 nest egg in order to provide the same buying power as we have today because of inflation. I am assuming that most working families will need at least $50,000 a year to live on in retirement. We don't know what will happen to Social Security by 2034. We don't know what employer pensions might look like by then. I am assuming that inflation will continue so planning is crucial to success in retirement.

Inflation will make the goods we buy now for $50,000 cost about $80,000. If Social Security or employer pensions can add to our basic income, that is fine. But we don't want to count on them. If there is a bad year like 2008, we are not taking money out of our growth funds at a bad time. The balanced fund has bonds which has traditionally been less volatile.

The funds we have listed above include some of the most consistent low volatility returns over time. Since our account is not taxable, there are no taxes when we take our monthly income later. We may not have to pay tax on our other income like Social Security and/or our qualified retirement funds. The gains on our account are tax-FREE after age 59.5. Unlike pensions and annuities, this account is tax-FREE. We pay $99,000 ($3,000 for 33 years) and $901,000 is FREE of tax.

The Keys to Wealth

1. **Costs matter**: Broker/advisor cost 1% to 3% every year

   If you use a salesperson, costs take HALF your money!
   $3,000 per year @11%   for 33 years = $1,018,177
   $3,000 per year @11-1% for 33 years = $778,768
   $3,000 per year @11-2% for 33 years = $613,805
   $3,000 per year @11-3% for 33 years = $486,634
   www.moneychimp.com/calculator/compound_interest_calculator.htm

2. Broker/advisor stock-picking does not beat index funds over time. No money manager has been able to beat the markets consistently. No one can forecast the future. http://investa.com/man-vs-machine-the-great-stock-showdown-wall-street-journal-05-10-13/

3. **Compounding** creates investment success; NOT buying and selling. The chance of you doing both, at the right times, is near zero. Warren Buffett's holding period is "forever." No trading!

4. A **tax-FREE** investment account increases your balance 30%.

5. Putting all your money in one stock or market sector guarantees failure over time. No one investment is perfect. Buy a **group of growing global businesses in a low-cost fund.**

6. 'Dollar cost average' buying technique lowers the cost of shares over time. When you invest a fixed amount each month, you buy more mutual fund shares when the price is low and less when high. Over time, you will own more shares at a lower average cost.

7. **Consistency** wins over the long term. Quick in and out trading only benefits Wall Street. Market timing may work for a short time but the odds of being right on the buy and sell are long.

8. **Patience** is required to allow your money to work for you. Building a business takes time. Investing is betting to most of us.

The DISRUPTORS help you build wealth

John Bogle, Warren Buffett and William Roth have changed our world. We can now complete an excellent financial plan in 1 hour. We can now earn 10-12% vs. 3.79% on our money. We can now use a proven LONG-TERM strategy so we take advantage of the most powerful investing force—compounding. We can now grow our account 10 times using the tax-FREE Roth IRA.

    Bogle proved cost matters. Buffett proved a simple market index beat the best Wall Street 'fortune tellers.' Sen Roth will be remembered for years. Compounding account earnings has been around since ancient Greece. Loaning money to a business over time so you can claim part of the profits is how the rich get and *stay* rich. Extra work is not necessary if we buy what we need.

    Fidelity found that the ***most successful investors*** were those that forgot their account or died. Most wealthy investors have learned patience is the Buffett secret to investing. They see how ***costs destroy*** their portfolio compounding. They avoid sales hype and use the strategy discussed above. That is why they stay rich.

    The industry has made building wealth a mystery so it can take $1.3 Trillion from our accounts year after year. The average advisor-run account return was only 3.79%. The fees buy toys for the Pimps of Wall Street. Over time that fee compounds our loss and can take up to 63% of our total possible accumulations. Advisors like to buy and sell creating taxes and fees.

    Advisors charge 1-3% whether they beat the averages or not. Advisors don't give refunds! The clear winning strategy is to use the 10 funds and let compounding work its magic. Over time using a tax-FREE account with low fees, we can accumulate $1,000,000 from $250 a month at 10-12%. Using a compounding calculator moneychimp.com/calculator/compound_interest_calculator.htm, we find the range is 31 to 35 years. If our spouse has an account, we can shorten the time to 26-29 years for a family $1 million.

    If we use an advisor, we may give up over $500,000 in total accumulations. Research has shown that the average investor actually earns just 3.79% not 11% annually over time.

    Our 10 funds for building wealth work because they are low-cost strategies inside a unique **tax-FREE trust account.** This eliminates the biggest killers of wealth: TAXES and FEES. We can be our own masters of tax-FREE wealth with patience. There is no need to pick stocks or hire expensive advisors or product pushers with hidden fees. We can do it ourselves as long as we have a plan. The plan is following Warren Buffett's strategy.

You must take the first step. Advisors can't profit from these steps. You have to call Vanguard or TIAA *yourself* to set up your account. It takes about 1 hour to set up a Roth IRA for each of you. You can do it online or by phone. You can begin with TIAA and $100 automatic contributions or Vanguard with $1,000. Put the contributions on automatic so you don't have to decide every month whether to invest. Future life happens and you want to be spending your $60-80,000 a year not praying Washington won't cut Social Security benefits every year.

If you have been investing, you can convert portions of your IRA each year, paying tax on the earnings as you go. Over time, your Roth account will grow with earnings that are tax-FREE. This money may reduce your overall tax in retirement. It also is a great estate planning tool since no tax will be due from your heirs either.

There is a clear reason why "working millionaires" become wealthy. It is not luck or inheritance. Millions of immigrants to this country have done it before. They lived below their means. They saved and invested in businesses. They did not let temporary cash flow problems stop them from building wealth. They used the same path to building wealth every day.

As many clients say, "I never even miss the contributions because I never see them. Then all of a sudden, I see my statement has $25,000, $50,000, $250,000, $1,000,000, $2,000,000. We are talking real money here."

The real secret to investing is **compounding**. Buffett says:

> "My wealth has come from a combination of living in America, some lucky genes, and **compound interest**."

Call Vanguard 800-551-8631 or TIAA **800-223-1200** today.

The Author

Ian Sender has been a financial services executive for over 20 years. He was a managing director of sales units of securities firms. He is one of the Insiders who contributed to the *The Insiders Guides* set of buyers' guides edited by Dan Keppel. Ian lives in New Jersey and the Caymans.

The Insiders' Guides to Buying Discount Financial Services: Buy Direct and Save $3,000 Every Year is available at Amazon, Barnes & Noble, Junglee, bookadda, allbookstores, ebay, fishpond, alibris, powells, booksamillion, etc

To receive Dan Keppel's weekly Alert, go to www.TheInsidersGuides.com

WHEN WILL YOU START YOUR TAX-FREE $1 MILLION ACCOUNT?

_____

_____

_____

www.ingramcontent.com/pod-product-compliance
Lightning Source LLC
Chambersburg PA
CBHW030039230526
45472CB00002B/594